Ginny The Little Blue Car is about **belonging** and the great feeling of finally getting picked.

This story has subthemes of personal self-worth, self-knowledge, patience and resilience. Consider these discussion questions for your young readers.

1. What stuck out to you about the story?
2. Where do you see belonging in the Ginny Book?
3. Have you ever felt like Ginny before?
4. Why should we be proud of Ginny?

To learn more about lessons with Ginny The Little Blue Car, to access coloring sheets for your students or to schedule and author visit email connect@thelionheartexperience.com

A premiere developing child resource from The Lion Heart Experience.

Known for his warmth, authenticity and quick connections with young people, Joe Vercellino and his dynamic team of performing artists are the premiere investment for schools looking to infuse a strong sense of self-worth into their students and educators. Starting as a street musician around the United States, and leaving his college experience with a degree in Music Education - Joe taught in Inner-City Detroit for ten years and was awarded the Teacher of The Year award for the City of Detroit from The Michigan Department of Education.

Leading a team of his past students and with a lasting impact on teens and teachers nationwide, The Lion Heart Experience creates tangible results in schools that are evident and felt by the community. Masterfully combining story, original music and visual-art together - Joe Vercellino and the Lion Heart Experience are the most refreshing and most needed message in schools today.

Learn more at thelionheartexperience.com

DREAM & HUSTLE

GINNY

The little blue car

By Joe Vercellino

Illustrated by Nicole Steffes

Dedicated to my grandmother, Virginia "Ginny" Attwood.
As well as to the last, the lost, the least and the looked over.

My name is **GINNY**
and I am a
little **BLUE** car.

Who would not want to be a car?

Cars see all **KINDS** of places,

HOT and cold,

BIG and small,

BUSY and quaint,

quiet and **LOUD**,

NEW and old.

This is what cars do, or so I'm told.

Some cars **BUZZ**,
PUTT, and **POP!**
Other cars **ZIP**,
ZOOM,
and never **STOP!**

I am a little **BLUE** car.

Can you see me?

I can drive **REAL** slow

right next to the beach.

Or I can drive you **FAST**

past **BIG** fields or city streets.

I am a car.

There's **NO PLACE** we can't reach.

I can do **ANYTHING**

because I am a car.

I can take you **NEAR**

and I can take you **FAR.**

I just have one problem...

No one has picked me off the car sales lot

Sometimes I wonder if I will **EVER** get to do what cars do.

Some of my friends say,

"**GINNY** is funny looking,"

or that I am too small or too blue.

But I know that I'm **PERFECT.**

There's **NOTHING** wrong with me.

I am a perfect blue car, someone will see!

Sometimes when it rains, my friends start to whine.

"It's too **WET** and too **COLD**," they say.

But I say the rain makes me **SHINE!**

The rain makes me **SMILE**

and cleans off the dust.

I just hope I don't

sit here too long,

I'm afraid I might rust.

Other **CARS** have families
to take to the **ZOO**.
They take them to **SCHOOL**;
they drive to the **POOL**.

STOP

They drive them
for **ICE CREAM**,
to the **MOVIES** and back.
They drive for a **TALK**
they drive to get **SNACKS**.

Cars drive for **DADS** and cars drive for **MOMS**,
cars drive for **SAD** people, **HAPPY,** or **CALM.**

Cars drive for big people and short people, too.

Cars are **GREAT** helpers whatever they do!

I can't wait for my chance; I hope it comes soon.

Someone will pick me; they will like **SMALL** and **BLUE.**

Now it's been DAYS,

WEEKS, even MONTHS.

Still no one to pick me.

No one to drive. Not even one.

FAMILIES come and visit,

they come for the day.

My heart comes **ALIVE**

when they look over my way.

They point **RIGHT** at me and say,

"THIS IS THE ONE!"

But I'm not who they pick

when the day is **ALL DONE.**

Now **FALL** has turned to **WINTER**

and winter has melted into **SPRING,**

my friends are all gone

and I am **STILL** here.

FALL
Festival

OCT 14-24

Still little **GINNY.**

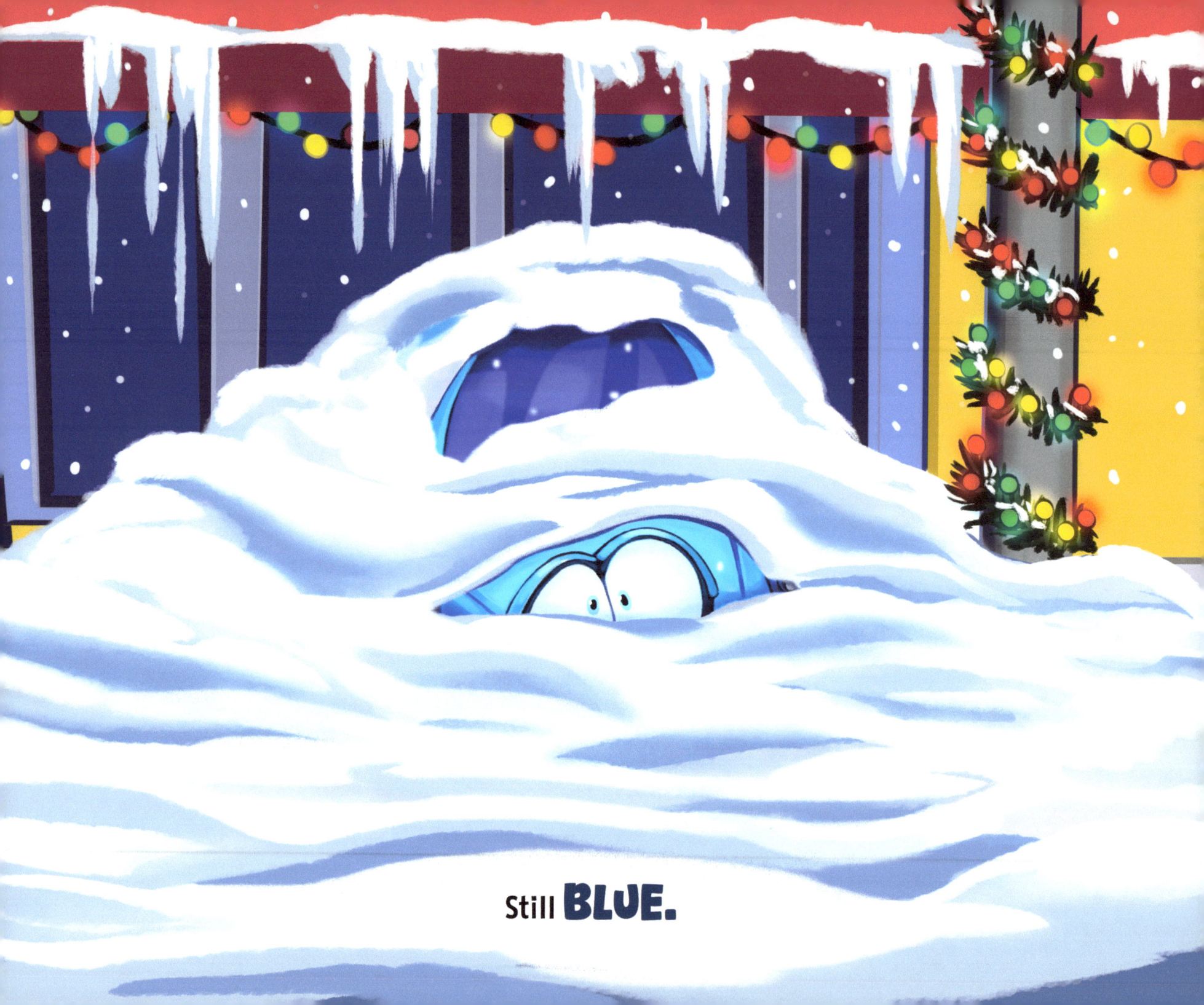

Still **BLUE.**

still WAITING.

Then on a **WARM** and **CLOUDY** mid-summer's day,

I know that I heard it. I heard someone say,

"What about that **BLUE** one? **THAT CAR** over there?"

said a man with a son with big curls in his hair.

The salesperson said,
"oh that **BLUE** car is too funny,
too blue, and **too small.**

Buying that car is not a good call. Come look over here!

You see, these cars **ZOOM,** these cars are **SPECIAL**, these cars are for you.

But they stayed and looked at me.

They opened my little **BLUE** doors.

They **DANCED** on my seats

and put their feet on my floors.

They rolled down my windows and I heard the dad say,

"we want this little **BLUE** car; we will buy it **TODAY**."

Off we drive,

my new **FAMILY** and I.

I'm so **HAPPY** they picked me.

They gave me a try! I waited and **HOPED**

and now my **DREAM** has come true,

The day is **FINALLY** here...

To do
what **CARS** do.

www.ingramcontent.com/pod-product-compliance
Lightning Source LLC
Chambersburg PA
CBHW042107090426

42811CB00018B/1872